Authenticity

Copyright © Argent (Property Development) Services LLP 2014
First published in Great Britain in 2015 by Argent (Property Development) Services LLP

The right of Antonia Higgs to be identified as the Author of the Work has been asserted by her in accordance with the Copyright, Designs and Patents Act 1988.

All rights reserved. No part of this publication may be reproduced, stored in a retrieval system, or transmitted, in any form or by any means, without the prior written permission of the publisher, nor be otherwise circulated in any form of binding or cover other than that in which it is published and without a similar condition being imposed on the subsequent purchaser.

All the characters in this publication are real and resemble living people.

A CIP Catalogue record for this book is available from the British Library.

ISBN 978-0-9931441-0-3

Typeset in Monotype Bembo
Designed and Illustrated by Sutton Young.
Printed and bound in England.

Argent (Property Development) Services LLP
4 Stable Street, King's Cross, London N1C 4AB

The paper this book is printed on is certified by the
© 1996 Forest Stewardship Council A.C. (FSC),
It is ancient-forest friendly.

Authenticity

Learning the art of making places

ANTONIA HIGGS

CONTENTS

CHAPTER 1	AUTHENTICITY	1
CHAPTER 2	URBAN CRISIS	7
CHAPTER 3	ROBUST URBAN FRAMEWORK	11
CHAPTER 4	ENGAGE AND INSPIRE	21
CHAPTER 5	A VIBRANT MIX	33
CHAPTER 6	A LASTING NEW PLACE	43
CHAPTER 7	MEANING IT	59
	ABOUT ARGENT	66
	HISTORY	67
	AWARDS	68

for everyone, everywhere

CHAPTER 1

AUTHENTICITY

Granary Square is a real place. It is on the map. It is authentic.

As the late summer sun warms the old railway sheds at King's Cross, thousands flock to London's coolest and newest public space: to dance in the fountains; to drape themselves on the bank of the canal; to flop in deckchairs; to meet and to eat; to drink and to think.

The commercial and the institutional spill happily into a free public realm. Sharp-suited workers from shiny offices step through family picnic parties as they look to seal some deal. Entrepreneurs, fresh off the Eurostar, pause to feel the vibe. Young lovers, curious pensioners, eager students and weary mums, travellers and locals, buskers and brokers – all are here.

Real places belong to everybody and nobody. They are the product of freedoms as much as of rules, of serendipity as much as of masterplans. Authenticity is begotten, not made.

Granary Square, barely two years old, has already been hailed as a masterpiece in the art of placemaking. The jewel in the crown of the admired King's Cross regeneration project, many come hoping

Canalside steps, Granary Square and the Granary Building - the heart of King's Cross

to discover its secrets, in order to practise the magic elsewhere. But there is no simple formula for success. Understanding why King's Cross works, and its implication for the development of great cities in the future, means taking a journey away from London and back in time. It means telling the story of one company, Argent, and its placemaking principles.

Founded in 1981 by two brothers, Michael and Peter Freeman, there has always been something slightly different about Argent. In an industry with a reputation for ruthless commercialism, these property developers sought to work with a sense of social responsibility and personal commitment that was ahead of its time. Argent has always wanted to make great places as well as great profits. Indeed, the company philosophy is that the two things go together.

The journey to Granary Square begins in Birmingham in the early nineties, moves on to Manchester and finally arrives in London with the new millennium; a tale of three cities in which Argent's inventive and principled approach to urban development develops and matures.

Argent's business values have helped it to become a key player in the great renaissance of English cities, with its belief in partnership and mixed use proving essential to the creation of successful commercial, residential and public spaces.

When selected in 2000 to develop King's Cross by the landowners and long-term investors, London and Continental Railways (LCR) together with logistics giant DHL, Argent felt it right to condense its philosophy into 'Principles for a Human City' – a document that has been seized upon as a foundation for urban regeneration policy.

Behind the ten short statements of intent lay weeks of expert evaluation, months of intensive consideration and years of sometimes bitter experience. They were an attempt to offer a pathway to great places yet to be, listing the aims that should, perhaps, guide any city developer:

A robust urban framework
A lasting new place
Promote accessibility
A vibrant mix of uses
Harness the value of heritage
Work for King's Cross, work for London
Commit to long-term success
Engage and inspire
Secure delivery
Communicate clearly and openly

From the conscientious application of these apparently straightforward principles, Argent and its partners have achieved something wonderfully complex. Real places.

Granary Square has become a popular destination for Londoners and visitors alike. King's Cross is a district being revived and reinvented as we watch.

But its importance for urban development is as a stop on a longer journey. This book attempts to explain how Argent has helped shape the art of placemaking in Britain, and how its principles might continue to inform the search for true authenticity.

Cafés bars and restaurants - Water's Edge, Brindleyplace

CHAPTER 2

URBAN CRISIS

In March 1988, groups of around a dozen men and women were invited to walk the few miles from Highbury Hall into the centre of Birmingham. Their starting point was the former home of the city's visionary 19th century mayor. Joseph Chamberlain was the man revered for rescuing Birmingham from a dystopian urban nightmare – 'badly lighted, imperfectly guarded, and only partially drained' – and turning it into a 'fine and open' Midland metropolis – 'parked, assized, marketed, gas and watered and improved'.

By the time they had completed their stroll, all were convinced that Birmingham was in desperate need of rescue once again. Participants in a symposium called 'The Highbury Initiative', the walkers described their city as a hostile environment, with an urban centre that was daunting, confusing, incoherent, with no emotional appeal.

One of the organisers of the weekend symposium was Councillor Sir Albert Bore, chairman of the city's economic development committee.

"It opened people's eyes up to what Birmingham city centre was," remembers Sir Albert, now leader of the city council. "It was a dying city in many respects."

Like many English cities cast in the furnaces of the industrial revolution, the collapse of the manufacturing businesses that had given it shape and purpose left Birmingham struggling to survive.

The economic crisis was made worse by disastrous planning policies from the 1960s that had seen concrete roadways slice through traditional urban communities. Social cohesion was sacrificed to the internal combustion engine. The Highbury Initiative described how the inner ring road had 'created a fortress island and a no man's land'.

"The city centre was constrained by the concrete collar of the inner ring road," Sir Albert explains. "There were physical and psychological barriers which meant it had no vibrancy, not much retail or leisure activity and virtually no-one lived there."

Those who could get out of central Birmingham did so, leaving behind a city with districts where over half the adult population was unemployed or sick. Barbed wire and CCTV attempted to keep order as squatters occupied deserted blocks, while prostitutes and drug dealers waited in the shadows.

"It was raw and it was dangerous," Argent Partner Roger Madelin recalls. Walking through a dingy and smelly pedestrian subway dishonestly named Paradise Circus, Madelin remembers his time as a student in Birmingham in the late seventies.

"It clearly was a city designed for cars but, as a young man from the South East, it was thrilling to go there and experience that urban, brutal environment," he says.

It wasn't just Birmingham. Across Britain the phrase 'inner city' had become shorthand for decline and menace; the word 'urban' associated with decay and danger. Communities were contaminated by crime in much the same way that the soil they lived upon was contaminated with the toxic residue of long-gone industry.

The exodus from city centres saw public spaces deserted, many becoming no-go areas for the law-abiding majority. Manchester's Piccadilly Gardens, once a source of horticultural pride at the heart of the city, won a reputation as a hangout for heroin addicts, flowerbeds prickling with hypodermic needles.

Argent Partner David Partridge remembers coming out of Manchester's main railway station to be presented with a place abandoned. "It was absolutely awful: a lot of it was completely derelict," he says. "The canal was choked with Japanese knotweed and swarming with rats." The only sign of human life was a billboard for cheap parking and an unappetising Indian restaurant. "That was your welcome to Manchester."

It was a similar story for passengers emerging at London's King's Cross station. The area, blighted by failed development schemes, had become a textbook example of urban decay. Soaring crime and vandalism had made its streets off-limits for most. Only pimps and pushers, clubbers and taxi drivers did much business. Graffiti on a wall at the back of the station reminded passers-by that this was the lawless district where the Director of Public Prosecutions, Sir Allan Green, had been arrested for kerb crawling.

"Frankly, people didn't care much for city centres at that time," Argent Partner Robert Evans remembers. A combination of financial deregulation, economic volatility and political tribalism had left many of Britain's cities with no sense of direction but down.

In 1992, Roger Madelin met Sir Albert Bore in Birmingham. "I said to Albert, 'This city is dying', and he agreed. Sometimes things have to get really bad before they can get better."

CHAPTER 3

ROBUST URBAN FRAMEWORK

In the early nineties, property developers had a significant image problem. Unfinished office blocks littering Britain's troubled city centres were seen as monuments to the greed of commercial speculators, to the tooth-and-claw capitalists who had strived to get rich quick in the unregulated trading environment after the Big Bang.

There was little sympathy in largely Labour-run cities for those who had lost everything when boom turned to bust. For many on the Left, developers were seen as foot soldiers of Thatcherism: far from offering a potential solution to urban decline, they were part of the problem. It was a caricature, of course, but in the fiercely tribal culture of British politics at that time, commercial property developers were deemed to have taken sides.

Such hostility was not felt by all, however. From the wreckage left by inner-city turmoil, a new type of city leader was emerging: ambitious, imaginative and, above all, pragmatic. Birmingham's Sir Albert Bore was among the first of this new breed.

"The city economy had collapsed but we had little access to Treasury funds because the Thatcher government weren't playing ball with us," Sir Albert says. "We desperately needed to get private sector investment, but Birmingham was not an attractive city."

In 1992, gloom threatened to become despair as a planned regeneration project promising to bring new homes and businesses to a run-down area of the city hit the buffers, with developers Rosehaugh falling victim to the property crash. Birmingham and Sir Albert were in a mess.

If Bore was a new breed of politician, Argent represented a different kind of developer. They both quickly realised that they shared the same aim: to make great places.

"When we met, we realised we were basically trying to do the same thing," Roger Madelin says. "You never really felt you were talking to a politician – you were talking to a custodian who wanted to improve the city."

The site for development, known as Brindleyplace, appeared distinctly unpromising. Seventeen acres of contaminated wasteland somewhere to the west of the city centre close to deprived areas of Ladywood, was how Argent assessed it. The foundries, mills and factories that once crowded along this section of the Grand Union Canal had long gone. It was now a toxic relic of Birmingham's manufacturing heritage, a miserable symbol of the city's industrial decline.

Yet from this unlikely plot would emerge a new approach to urban development that would be copied and adapted in cities across the country.

Originally conceived as a huge commercial and leisure development, Birmingham's ambitious masterplan for Brindleyplace now included public squares, restaurants, shops and bars overlooking the canals, as well as 120 new homes intended to encourage people to move back into the city. Many of the radical ideas for reinvigorating Birmingham's core that had emerged from The Highbury Initiative were incorporated in the city's vision for Brindleyplace. It all added to the risk, taking most developers out of their comfort zone. But Argent recognised an opportunity.

For all its challenges, Brindleyplace was a rare thing: a site in a major city under a single owner with planning permission and vacant possession. It was, Argent's board concluded, the opportunity of a lifetime.

If they really believed in creating great urban places, this was the chance to prove it.

Argent put in a bid of just over £3m, a fraction of what Roschaugh had paid just a year earlier, but the new proposal embraced Birmingham's vision for a mixed-use city centre development.

Argent's pitch was founded upon some of the principles that would be codified a decade later for King's Cross. It talked of creating a lasting new place with a commitment to the long-term, of a vibrant mix of uses within a scheme that would harness the heritage of the area, engaging and inspiring local people.

It was music to Sir Albert's ears. "What you had was a coming together of similar minds, from the public sector in terms of the city council and the private sector in terms of Argent," Sir Albert says.

The word 'placemaking' was rarely heard in 1992, but Argent's strategy for Brindleyplace rested on just that, chiming with Birmingham's own radical vision for the site. Its business model was about creating a diverse community in a vibrant urban space.

The first priority was delivering new public realm and 'destination' uses along the 'Water's Edge'.

"We start with the presumption that creating the nicest place will in due course be the most valuable place," Madelin explains. "Brindleyplace was the first site I know of where the developer said 'Why not?'"

As public and private working together, Birmingham and Argent started challenging conventional urban development ideas. The scheme included office buildings mixed with restaurants, an art gallery and Sea Life Centre; big retail chains were turned away in favour of local independent shops and restaurants and, most ambitious of all, the council had agreed that a residential community, Symphony Court, should be part of the plans. While commentators were predicting the death of the city centre and a shift towards out-of-town business, retail and residential zones, Brindleyplace was doing the opposite.

Designers, architects, planners and other local authorities were intrigued. Busloads of students arrived to try to understand what the council and Argent were up to, how mixed use worked on the ground.

"I went on a minibus tour in the early nineties," Robert Evans reveals. As a geography student, the future Argent Partner had been fascinated by the claims made for the Birmingham scheme, particularly the idea that people would want to move back into the inner cities.

"I remember going to Brindleyplace and marvelling at the ambition of the scheme, particularly Symphony Court. It seemed so brave, even with the gates that would raise eyebrows today." A BBC news report at the time interviewed one of Symphony

Court's first residents asking why anyone would want to move back into the city centre and where would you buy a pint of milk? "The implication was that choosing urban living made you a bit odd," Evans recalls.

Brindleyplace, though, quickly established itself as a success. The Environment Secretary John Gummer talked enthusiastically about the approach. "Development is more sustainable if it produces a mixtures of uses," he told a conference in 1995. "Segregation of land uses, encouraged in the past, is not relevant now."

Although the circumstances behind Brindleyplace were not going to be replicated exactly in other cities, people began looking to Birmingham for clues as to how to bring vitality back to the moribund brownfield sites that stained once proud industrial cities.

"Every city had to have a Brindleyplace," says Argent Partner David Partridge. "It was really shorthand for saying you wanted a piece of imaginative urban design, and that is what Howard was looking for in Manchester."

Like Sir Albert Bore in Birmingham, Sir Howard Bernstein was a man determined to breathe new life into the city he loved. After the IRA detonated 1,500 kilos of explosive in central Manchester on Saturday 15th June 1996, the city turned to him to repair, to rebuild and to renew. As the city's chief executive he had a reputation as a shrewd pragmatist as well as a visionary thinker.

"What the bomb allowed us to do was to think radically," Sir Howard explains. "How do we re-plan the city? How do we strengthen functionality? How do we create more commercial opportunities? How do we create places where people feel safe and comfortable?"

Sir Howard took stock and concluded that, although parts of Manchester were thriving, other districts were struggling badly, holding back the city's fortunes. One such central neighbourhood was the gateway for thousands of workers and shoppers deposited by bus and tram each day: Piccadilly Gardens. Once a jewel in the city's crown, the area had become, in Sir Howard's understated view, "very tired".

He announced a competition to develop the sunken gardens and revive this key location. Once again stressing its commitment to placemaking, Argent emerged as the winner.

"The council and Argent's partnership was driven by a clear understanding and a shared view about place – what made places work, why people choose to live and work in places," Sir Howard says.

It was a nod to the skills Argent had honed in Brindleyplace, a flexible approach that meant challenging convention.

"What Argent identified in Birmingham, and then moved on in Manchester, was a model for how you transform really complex spaces that involve public realm and private landowners," Partridge believes.

The company's first project in Manchester involved a landmark office building in the centre of the city, but linked to the regeneration of the public gardens next door. As in Birmingham, the project would reflect Argent's commitment to mixed use. The office building became home to the Bank of New York Mellon, but at street level it included a range of retail outlets, shops and restaurants that helped animate the whole area. Argent established and led the Piccadilly Partnership – a group of stakeholders from public and private sectors, working together to make the area prosperous and attractive. Piccadilly Gardens themselves, once a virtual no-go area, were reclaimed as one of Manchester's most visited places, some 18 million people strolling through each year.

"We didn't just look at it as real estate," David Partridge says. "We looked at it as a great opportunity to transform part of a city – not from the outside in but from the inside out." It was this philosophy that led to Argent later being selected as development partner for further projects in and around the Piccadilly area of Central Manchester; and most recently at One St. Peter's Square.

Argent's partnership approach, the principles which underpin its business model and the concept of placemaking are now seen as key components of the urban renaissance that has turned around the fortunes of a number of English cities and will continue to do so. It is a model that hinges on a trusting relationship between commercial developers and city leaders.

When Argent was selected by LCR and DHL as developer for the huge King's Cross project in 2000, it recognised that the social and political importance of this complex scheme would test those qualities to the full.

"There was a lot of suspicion then within the local authority," Robert Evans remembers. "Some of the local politicians would literally cross the street to avoid having to speak to us. To be seen with a developer was almost like a crime, I suppose. It offended their sensibilities."

After its experiences in Birmingham and Manchester, however, Argent knew that building a positive relationship with the local council was vital.

On the day Argent got the contract, Madelin wrote to the leader of Camden Council, Jane Roberts, the local authority which would have to grant planning permission for the whole project. To his amazement, the next morning his telephone rang. "It was one of the most embarrassing conversations I have ever had," Madelin admits. "She said 'It's Jane Roberts'. I said, 'Who?' 'I am the leader of Camden Council. You wrote to me yesterday.'"

Jane Roberts was amused at Madelin's embarrassment. "I rang him straight back because why on earth wouldn't you? It was my responsibility as leader to engage and look them directly in the eyes."

Argent realised it was dealing with another of the new breed of leader. Like Sir Albert Bore in Birmingham, Jane Roberts was a pragmatist trying to cut a path through the tangled briars of political tribalism.

"For me, it was the politics that needed to be sorted," Roberts says. "I was really clear on the aspirations. This was a fantastic opportunity that we couldn't blow, for Camden, for London and for the country, to have a thriving, buzzy, kind, interesting place that looked good, felt good and had things we needed."

It was a vision for King's Cross that matched Argent's own ambitions, but it was clear that many in Jane Roberts' own party were unconvinced.

Argent decided to try to start building a consensus by spelling out its philosophy, to put down on paper the ethos that underpinned the work it was doing in Manchester and Birmingham, and against which it wished to be held to account. After a series of workshops with the emerging team, in July 2001 Argent distilled its thinking and published 'Principles for a Human City'.

"Our objective for King's Cross Central is to devise and then deliver, over the next 15 or so years, an exciting and successful mixed use development; one that will shape a dense, vibrant and distinctive urban quarter, bring local benefits and make a lasting contribution to London," the document stated, before setting out the ten principles.

Camden Council and English Heritage both contributed forewords to the 'Principles for a Human City' which have framed more than a decade's work on 'successful and sustainable urban renewal'. The principles are widely referenced in other projects, above all perhaps, because they recognise that, while such projects involve competing interests, all parties benefit from creating 'a human city'. The prize is authenticity.

Children play, fountains bubble and dance - Granary Square

CHAPTER 4

ENGAGE AND INSPIRE

The principles that underpin Argent's approach to placemaking began to take shape in those early days working on Brindleyplace. The radical ideas for the site were devised in partnership with Birmingham's leaders, but local people were far from persuaded.

"We had a problem in getting the public to understand and agree what we were doing because it was out of keeping with how they saw Birmingham," says Sir Albert Bore. "Birmingham was regarded as a brash manufacturing city, but the experience of Brindleyplace proved to be the lever to changing the public mindset."

Sir Albert says Argent helped 'retune' local people's ambition for their city.

"It certainly wasn't easy to engage because we were seen as the enemy." Roger Madelin remembers the suspicion and distrust felt by local people in Birmingham at the arrival of 'fancy-pants developers' on their doorstep in the early nineties. "I went to a meeting at a nearby community centre and someone got up and said, 'Mr Madelin is talking about all this investment and all these jobs. None of the jobs are for us. No-one here works there.'"

It was to be a familiar complaint – developers seeking to enrich themselves at the expense of local people. The project appeared to belong to outsiders who didn't understand the character of the place. Argent's response then was exactly as it is today – to try to engage.

"All you can do is be open, be accessible and be straight with people," Robert Evans says. "Don't promise what you can't do and if you do say you will do something, do it."

Argent attempted to communicate its vision for the project at public meetings and events, often having to explain or defend the property development business to sceptical audiences.

"We were just very open with people about how the system works and what we were doing," Madelin says. "It doesn't always get them on your side but it stops them being completely hostile."

When a TV reporter asked Madelin when work on Brindleyplace would begin, he replied that it would start on 6th September. "People were horrified," he recalls. "'Why did you give them a date?', they asked. 'Because that's when we are going to start', I said. And we did. Building that credibility was a good first step."

Gradually, as the work progressed, suspicion turned to curiosity and, ultimately, to pride in Brindleyplace. "I used to go down there and eavesdrop and, as the development happened, you could perceptibly feel the change in attitude and hear it in what people were saying," Sir Albert says. "You got people bringing their friends or families down just to show them what was happening."

In May 1998, on the balcony of the Malt House pub overlooking the refurbished iron bridges and restored waterways, Bill Clinton drank a pint of beer. Taking time out from the G8 Summit, the US President toasted Brindleyplace.

It was a lesson in long-term community relations which Argent built upon when they became the selected developer for the huge King's Cross project in 2000. Their commitment to 'engage and inspire' articulated in 'Principles for a Human City' began with a quotation from Lord Scarman, who reported on the race riots in Brixton in 1981: "When people feel they 'belong' to a neighbourhood which is theirs through their own efforts, then it will become a place ... worth struggling to retain and develop."

Argent recognised that simply engaging with all its neighbours around the site, never mind inspiring them, was going to be an enormous undertaking. The scale and complexity of the project meant that there were myriad community associations, pressure groups, societies and sceptical individuals to get to know.

Between them, Roger Madelin, Robert Evans and other team members attended literally hundreds of community and society meetings, an exercise that was time-consuming but critically important.

"They did a lot of very good work," says Angela Inglis, a writer and photographer who campaigned to protect the historical legacy of the King's Cross site. "They came round to my house and looked at my photographs and I alerted them to the importance of the gasholders."

The story of the Victorian gasholders reflects the care and thought Argent and Camden Council gave to their responsibilities in developing King's Cross. Originally constructed in the 1850s, the gasholders had become a familiar symbol of the site's industrial history.

"I was particularly interested in the gasholders because of their intricate embellishments and their magnificent latticed frames,"

Inglis explains. "Whenever I photographed them, people passing would stop to talk with me about their elegant structure and how it would not be King's Cross without them."

Argent took such views on board. The listed gasholder guide frames were to be dismantled and then painstakingly refurbished before being moved to a new home close to the canal. Gasholder No. 8 would sit in a landscaped setting and frame a new park. The three largest gasholders (Nos. 10, 11 and 12) known as 'The Siamese Triplets' would be the inspiration for a dramatic residential development within the footprint of the re-erected frames, a solution that added significantly to the cost but was true to Argent's principles.

"They have done the right thing with the gasholders," Inglis says, although this tough campaigner still has misgivings about some other aspects of the scheme. "They spent a lot of time talking to people but, as far as I was concerned, they didn't take enough notice of it!"

Much of the local community concern centred on protecting the character and history of the area. Argent's commitment to 'harness the value of heritage', one of its ten principles, recognises a balance between conserving the historic environment and the benefits of development.

Argent and local councils agreed at an early stage to support and encourage community groups and those living and working in the area to have their say. The King's Cross Development Forum was set up by the council and local people so that concerned individuals and bodies could help shape the future of their neighbourhood. Trips were arranged around the site and to other developments and independent expertise provided in the shape of Planning Aid for London, so that residents could inform themselves about the potential of the project.

ENGAGE AND INSPIRE

The gateway to King's Cross - Battle Bridge Place

"Tall buildings are OK; fishing and walking must be protected; they should try to retain the old Victorian sheds; affordable housing south of the canal; shock at there being a basis for developers making a profit" – the minutes from an early meeting give a flavour of the views expressed.

It was clear that it would be impossible to please all the people all the time, but Argent recognised that having supportive communities around the site would make the project run more smoothly and ultimately make the area more valuable. "Cities are complicated places with lots of different types of people in them," Robert Evans says. "That is what makes urban development so challenging, but it is also what makes sustainable places with enduring value."

Although it might not always win every argument, Argent believed it was critical that local people still felt that their views and passions mattered. One early disagreement with the Development Forum was over the future of existing social housing on the site, in particular a block of Victorian apartments built for railway workers known as the Culross Buildings. "I was so sad when they knocked down Culross", Angela Inglis remembers. "I was allowed to go and take all the photographs of the demolition. I don't know why they allowed me to do that."

While some shed a tear, others believe Argent has achieved a good balance between restoration and development.

"They have taken down a lot of the old crud and they have conserved some of the most interesting bits of industrial architecture. I think that was the right thing to do," London Mayor Boris Johnson asserts. "The classic success of London regeneration is when you get the old traditional brick Victorian buildings and then intensify their interest by putting some snazzy piece of architecture next door – both look better by proximity to the other. That is what you see at King's Cross. People like the mixture."

Having been appointed to develop Piccadilly Place in 2002, David Partridge wanted Manchester to be proud of what had been an embarrassing eyesore right outside the main railway station.

"The question we asked ourselves was, 'How do we make people feel that this project is for them?'", Argent Partner David Partridge says. "We held a competition called 'Poem for Manchester' in which people had to write a haiku about why they love the city."

The Poet Laureate at the time, Andrew Motion, selected twelve of the entries which were displayed around the city and then there was a public vote. The winning entry is engraved into the fabric of the Piccadilly Place development.

"It involved the whole city for weeks," Partridge remembers. "It was great. We had schoolkids doing open mic sessions with people booing and cheering. We promoted through local media and on the sides of buses. It was about being part of a city."

When Argent telephoned the winner Mike Duff to congratulate him, he said the competition had made his life. "I feel as though I'm being honoured by the city and that I will become a permanent part of it," he told the press. "That is worth more than money to me."

Nearly 10 years later, the 'Poem for Manchester' was the inspiration for another public competition in King's Cross. The London development is creating some twenty new streets and more than ten public spaces that all need names. Some were obvious. Stable Street was on the site of stabling for thousands of horses used to take goods off the trains during the station's Victorian heyday; Granary Square was outside the existing Granary building. But Argent and its partners decided to involve the general public in deciding what the others should be called.

"What occurs to you is that, while the buildings may come and go, the streets and the squares could very well be here in 500 years' time," Argent Partner Nick Searl points out. "If you believe in cities, and we do, you have to take such responsibilities seriously."

Argent published a detailed report explaining the process and the history of the site. When an open competition was launched on the company website, it attracted a remarkable 10,000 suggestions. "There was a bit of a campaign for Amy Winehouse Street but, although she had quite a lot to do with Camden, there are few links with King's Cross," Robert Evans reveals. "The competition is definitely not X Factor; it's not a popularity contest but we have learned so much about our own site. The competition has engaged people and they have come up with some fantastic names that we are now using."

Former Camden Council leader Jane Roberts, a local school governor, heard about the competition and encouraged the pupils to have a go. "I saw it as a chance to give them a sense of ownership in what was happening on their doorstep," she says. "It would be so great if a youngster walking around the area saw a street name and thought 'I suggested that!'"

It would have been more straightforward simply to have sought the advice of council archivists or historical experts, but time and again during the development, Argent has sought to stimulate community participation and involvement.

Normally, once construction has begun, developers tend to put a high fence around a site to keep people out. But, while conscious of the safety issues, Argent tries to do the opposite – seeking at ways to bring local people in.

"Very early in the process at King's Cross, we invited the public to walk through the site," Searl says. "We built a route through with a square, which was quite risky from a business perspective because the site wasn't producing any revenue at that stage. But what it does is it involves people. It makes them feel part of the process – they see this place evolving around them every day. And they are excited."

When a local charity, Global Generation, approached Argent about its work with young people building gardens and growing food, Argent immediately recognised the benefits. "It is about engaging with kids, giving them confidence, helping them develop skills," Evans explains. "We decided the garden should be in skips, so that we could move them around, to undeveloped areas of the site. They've occupied three locations already." The skips not only grow food that is sold to local restaurants, they spawned the Skip Garden Café – an example of organic development. "Nobody would have predicted that, but you can't help but smile. They are just along from Google Glass and what will be Waitrose. It's why we love cities. It's serendipity."

Argent continues to organise tours and competitions for pupils at nearby secondary schools. They provide a chance for youngsters to learn about the scheme on their doorstep, and a learning opportunity for Argent too. "What I see in that process is children from homes where neither parent has ever worked, without ambition. It opens your eyes to the challenge," Searl acknowledges. "If we can create a dialogue with young people and raise their ambition, that is extraordinary and about as much as a developer can ever hope to achieve."

Argent's published 'principles' for King's Cross placed particular emphasis on engaging with children and young people. 'They will live with – and hopefully benefit from – the redevelopment over the next 10 to 20 years,' the document pointed out. It was a commitment that took the developers into new areas.

As part of the planning approval for King's Cross, Argent agreed to build a new primary school at the heart of the site – interestingly the school will also be co-located with Frank Barnes School for Deaf Children. As an academy operating outside local authority control, the primary school needed an outside sponsor.

"We thought, hang on a minute, who is best placed to give the school every advantage in terms of its neighbours, its business links, all the things the school wants to lean on in terms of outreach?" Robert Evans recalls. "Who is best placed? Us."

For Argent, King's Cross Academy represented an opportunity to prove that it saw development as far more than bricks and mortar. The application to become the school's sponsor was a demonstration of one of its ten principles: 'commit to long-term success'. In February 2014, the Department for Education agreed that Argent, as part of the 'King's Cross Central Limited Partnership', should establish and operate a primary school.

"It is slightly daunting, I will confess, and there is a lot to learn," admits Evans, who is now the head of governors. Argent founder Michael Freeman and his wife Clara are also members of the Academy Trust. "By the time we come to the end of the King's

Cross project in 2020, the first intake of children will be preparing for secondary school," Evans points out. "In a sense, our school will be a measure of its success as a regeneration project."

A place to sit, a place to chat - Central Square

CHAPTER 5

A VIBRANT MIX

From Brindleyplace to Granary Square, a key feature of Argent's approach to urban regeneration is mixed use. In 1992, when Birmingham City Council and Argent adopted a masterplan that included residential, retail and office development, it heralded a new era for city development. Central to Britain's urban renaissance is the belief that sustainability, vibrancy and authenticity can only come from creating places that belong to all.

"King's Cross is a slice of the city, a big slice, and within that slice one should find all urban life," Robert Evans believes. "Mix is good. Rather than having a monoculture of age or tenure or type, we just think the mix is healthy to make the place: top-end apartments and social housing; a Michelin star restaurant and a place to buy chips and beans for £3.99."

It is a philosophy, of course, which chimes with government demands that urban development should reduce inequality and strengthen communities – providing homes and jobs for local people as well as creating a prosperous business environment. But it is a balance that is always controversial.

"There were big arguments about it," Jane Roberts recalls. As leader of Camden council when planning approval for King's Cross Central was under discussion, she remembers the suspicion of local politicians. "It was a mixture of, 'We can't trust these people', 'We want more affordable housing', 'We want the buildings preserved', 'We don't want too many office blocks' …"

It was a long and involved negotiation, but Roberts became convinced that Argent was genuine in its commitment to creating a place that offered both lasting economic and social value.

"We liked what we saw of Argent, but we were going to stick up for what we felt was right and what we felt would fit in," she says. "I wanted something that felt and looked really good, that had a high proportion of affordable housing. That's how you make communities work – they need to be mixed."

From the outset, Argent had committed to providing a range of private and affordable housing. 'If King's Cross is to become an exemplar for London as a sustainable world city,' they had said, 'we must provide a variety of homes.' A deal on the mix of housing provision was made just as the storm clouds of what would prove to be a global recession were gathering.

"After the world turned in 2008, many developers went back and renegotiated contracts," Evans notes. "But we didn't do that. We stuck to the deal."

In fact, affordable housing was the first residential stock to be built. Rubicon Court, to the north of the site, was completed in the glorious Olympic summer of 2012, delivering 117 affordable homes in partnership with the housing association One Housing

Group. Shortly afterwards, Saxon Court and Roseberry Mansions added a further 143 affordable units.

Visitors are struck by the quality of the provision and the attention to detail: burgundy brickwork in Rubicon's entrance lobby echoing the old Metropolitan underground station on the other side of the road; elegant spandrels and balustrades on Saxon speaking of a building that is valued.

The housing is designed to be tenure blind – it shouldn't be obvious which blocks are private or affordable. And within the buildings one finds social rented, shared ownership, even extra-care accommodation for the elderly and those with mental health needs.

The ArtHouse Building, with its fabulous views across the city, provides private homes to the highest standards. But even in this block are affordably-priced apartments that look identical from the outside to the up-market neighbours.

"This isn't about doing something soft-hearted or trying to be nice to the council," Evans insists. "King's Cross is more sustainable, more valuable through that richness and diversity. It is multi-faceted, it is layered, it is complicated – that's what great British cities are like."

Unlike the 'grand projet' of Haussmann's Paris or the grid-rigid geometry of New York, London is a city of accidents. Its streets and buildings, its parks and squares, have simply evolved over time, incorporated through centuries of contradiction and irrationality.

It is a similar story in Manchester and Birmingham. The great metropolitan centres of England are a jumble of history and happenstance, an unlikely consequence of fire and flood, bombs and bankruptcy.

"That is the strength and weakness of British cities – we haven't let central planning dictate, except perhaps in the sixties when we let highway planners run amok and destroy places with ring roads," Evans reflects. "Central planning has never been a dominant influence on London. That's part of its charm, that mercantile influence, the make-do-and-mend quality."

Rich cheek-by-jowl with poor, barrowboys rubbing shoulders with bankers: mix has always been part of Britain's urban DNA, places founded upon compromise and negotiation, trust and partnership.

"We have to understand and respect each other's perspectives." Manchester's Chief Executive Sir Howard Bernstein believes that the relationship he had with Argent not only challenged the developer in terms of social benefit, but the local authority in terms of its responsibilities.

"The Piccadilly Partnership, that Argent led, became a model for city centre management that you now see in many parts of the country."

Prompted by Argent, developers, landowners, businesses and the local authority sat together under the banner of the Piccadilly Partnership. "We all wanted Manchester to be a world-class international city, but having landowner and business involvement gave specific perceptions about the role and contribution each could make to the overall vision, very different questions uniquely discussed in Manchester at that time."

What Argent began in Birmingham and refined in Manchester was a way to mirror the complexity of the city in a group of people who could make things happen. The mix was reflected in partnership. "As soon as we set up the Piccadilly Partnership, the area acquired a personality very different from its reputation for drugs and prostitution," David Partridge explains.

It was a perception that drove the reality. From what was a dangerous and neglected neighbourhood opposite Manchester's main railway station emerged Piccadilly Place, an Argent development of offices, shops and homes. "We recognise the importance of achieving a balance of uses in creating great places," Partridge says. "This corner of the city is beginning to come back to life again."

It is indeed. One Piccadilly Place is now the landmark DoubleTree by Hilton hotel. Next door is the headquarters of Transport for Greater Manchester. Across the way, more than 300,000 sq ft of top grade office and retail space has as its neighbour a block of stylish and contemporary apartments known as The Hub. The buildings border a privately-managed piazza that has become a popular location for street parties and festivals.

"Argent understands the quality of design," Sir Howard says. "Spaces matter to them – not just because it's the best way to maximise their profit margins, but also because of the contribution it makes to community and place. There is a very genuine commitment to that."

The partners at Argent take that commitment very seriously. Central to the company's success has been its ability to convince planning authorities that it is sincere in wanting to create vibrant communities and lasting places.

"The argument that had been played out in London planning policy about places like King's Cross for 30-40 years is, 'What is the land for?'" Robert Evans asserts. "Is it to meet a city's needs or is it about

The place to meet and greet - Piccadilly Gardens

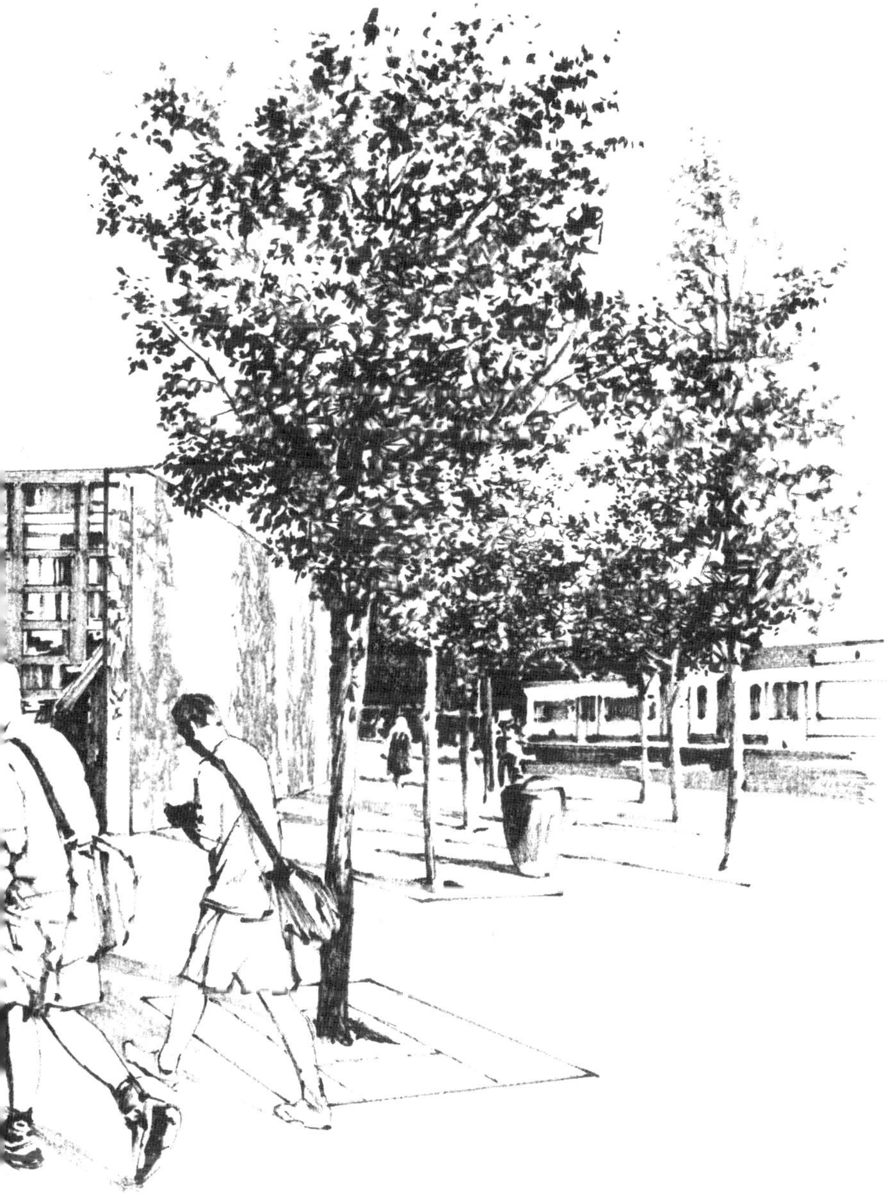

local needs? Is it about the demands of the central business district or about affordable homes and local jobs? The answer is of course 'both', and the exact combination is what the debate has been about."

The very first building put up on the King's Cross site was a construction skills academy, a high-specification training facility three times as big as originally demanded by Camden Council. It was an important statement of intent, sending a message about the high status Argent gives to the construction industry, but also about its determination to provide jobs on the site for local people.

"We think that's good business," Argent Construction Partner Tony Giddings explains, "because if you are doing a 13-year building project, having skilled labour that's on hand makes a lot of sense."

A decade earlier, at Brindleyplace in Birmingham, Argent had found itself challenged by local people on why it seemed the development was not providing jobs for them. Often the answer was that the young unemployed on the neighbouring estates simply did not have the skills required, but it threatened to fuel local resentment as they endured the disruption on their doorstep.

It was an issue that both Argent and Camden Council were keen to address at King's Cross.

"We had a responsibility to protect the interests of the neighbouring estates where residents don't traditionally make a fuss and who were going to suffer years of dust and lorries," says Jane Roberts. "The site needed to provide opportunities for them in terms of jobs and training."

The target agreed how many of the jobs on site should be taken up by local people and has proved to be a challenge. The skills centre certainly hums with activity, but there has always been a question as to whether the facility is there to help the most job ready into work or to be a social project focusing on the hardest to reach. "The fact that we haven't always hit the target reflects the ambition of the target," Evans argues. "Besides, regeneration is a partnership. Camden and Islington have a huge part to play on the 'supply side' and they employ the training provider, as well as lease the centre. We and our contractors represent the demand side. It's about working together."

A quiet life amongst the limes - Granary Square

CHAPTER 6

A LASTING NEW PLACE

Placemaking is an art more than a science. Having been selected to breathe new life into London's internationally important King's Cross area, Argent sought inspiration. The team gathered a little over a mile south of the station, in a spot that had been inspiring the capital's population for centuries.

They met in the Courthouse of St. Andrew in Holborn. Through the high-arched Gothic-style windows, the team could see the church designed by Sir Christopher Wren after the Great Fire. In fact, Londoners had been coming to this site looking for spiritual enlightenment and wisdom for much longer than that; there had been a place of worship on the site since medieval times and excavation work had just revealed that the Romans had been in occupation.

Where better to contemplate the task in hand, turning a neglected slice of this great metropolis into a lasting new place?

Argent organised a series of lectures and workshops with the team that would shape King's Cross: amongst them Arup, Allies and Morrison, Demetri Porphyrios and Robert Townshend. Demetri Porphyrios presented a masterclass on the history of planning settlements since Roman times. Porphyrios, an architect and classicist who had worked with Argent for over ten years, encouraged his audience to turn contemporary development practice on its head.

"The lectures inspired Argent to think differently," says partner Nick Searl. Although he joined the company later, the legacy of those seminars is retained in the way that Argent thinks about place. "Don't worry about the buildings for a minute, look at the city. What is the experience of people arriving here? How will they move through the area? Where will they go? What will draw them on their route? Where will they stop?"

Normally, developers put together a masterplan for a site by first locating the key buildings, calculating the potential value of each property in each position. Once that is agreed, they work out how best to use the public spaces in between.

This approach starts with the public realm, considering the best layout of streets and squares before deciding where the buildings should go. The theory owes much to the ideas of Giambattista Nolli, an 18th century Italian architect and surveyor best known for his map of Rome in which buildings and space are inverted – space marked black and buildings left white.

"If you think like that, the spaces become the object and the buildings become subservient to the space," Searl suggests. "As an architecture student you learn about Nolli plans, but then you go off to work and do the exact opposite. You get seduced into thinking it's all about buildings and then wonder why places don't hang together."

The lectures at St. Andrew's were not the first time Argent had been presented with a Nolli approach to urban development. Sir Terry Farrell's masterplan for Brindleyplace in Birmingham was, in the words of Argent partner David Partridge, "essentially about spaces with buildings around them".

The Highbury Initiative that had spawned the city's regeneration in the late eighties envisaged a network of pedestrian routes or trails across the city, challenging the hegemony of the motorcar. "Along these pedestrian routes efforts must go into improving the environment," the Highbury symposium document had concluded, "and a collaborative effort will be needed between public agencies and private property owners."

The key, therefore, was the public realm – the streets and pathways, the squares and parks that would lead people through the urban jungle. "The first thing to do when Argent bought the site at Brindleyplace was to choose the designer of the urban spaces," Partridge says.

For the central square, they agreed with Robert Townshend a design that included fountains and pools built around curving steps and grass, hinting at an amphitheatre for public events. A sculpture was commissioned, public art that would echo the 'genius' of Brindleyplace. Miles Davies' 'Aqueduct' resonates with the history of Birmingham's canals, of iron and of industry.

Only after the layout of the public square had been decided did Argent organise a competition for the buildings that would frame it. Four architects, working in isolation, were asked to produce a 1:200 cardboard mock-up of their design and finally, at an extraordinary event in the offices of the project engineers, each placed their model around a scaled layout of the square.

A place to be - Central Square

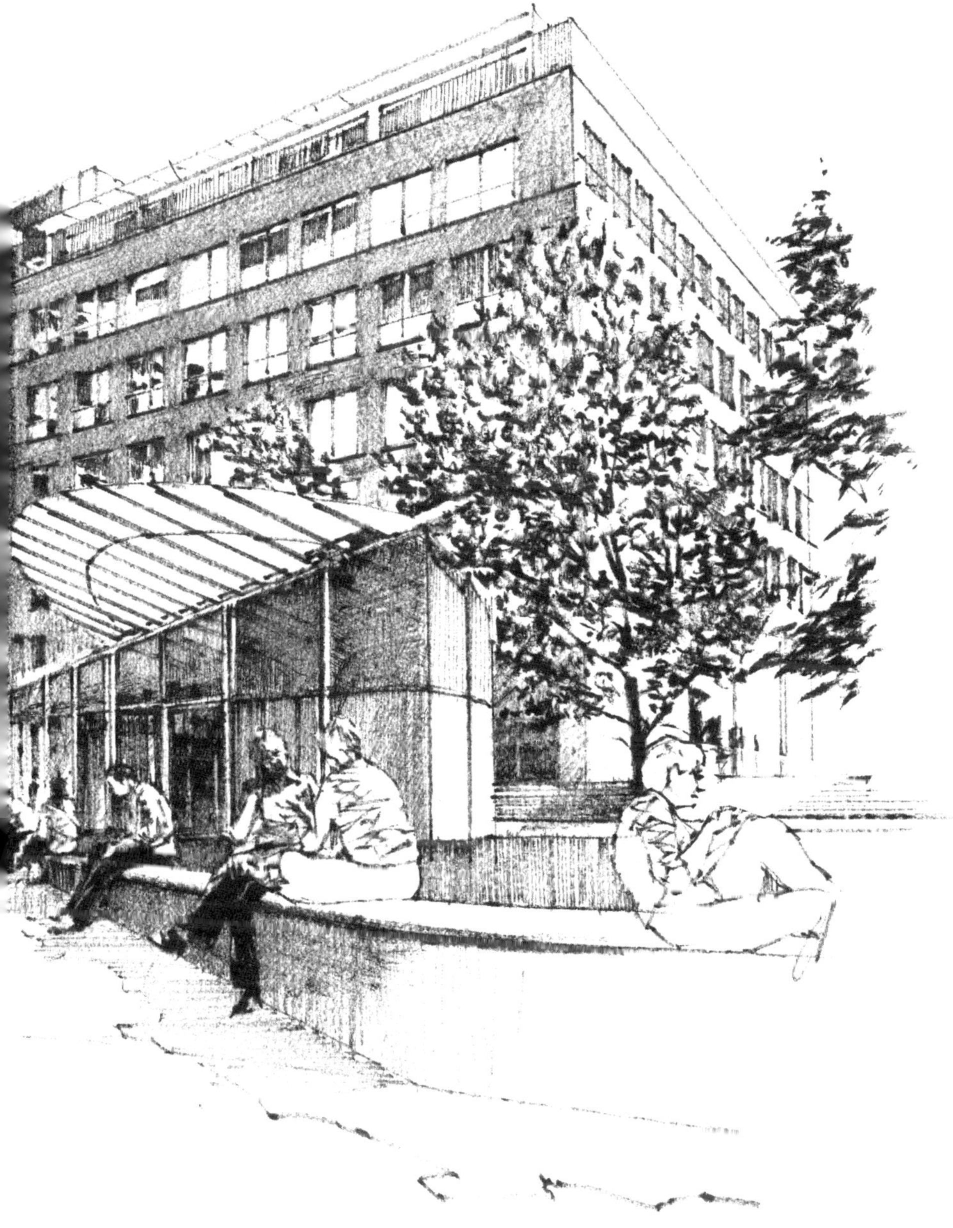

It was a remarkable exercise that reflects Argent's profound and continued commitment to the importance of public space.

Once completed, Central Square achieved more than Argent could have hoped. Families came and laid out their rugs and ate picnics. Amused office workers looked out at children skipping in the fountains. The square hummed with chatter and laughter.

A few years later in Manchester, Argent achieved a similar outcome for Piccadilly Gardens. An area that had been almost off-limits was restored as a vibrant and attractive civic space.

In thinking about their approach to King's Cross, the lectures at St. Andrew's Courthouse kept returning to what Argent was doing in Birmingham and in Manchester. "We spent a lot of time asking how other masterplans had worked," Robert Evans recalls. "The team inverted our King's Cross plans, making the spaces black and the buildings white, we looked at connections, the spaces, the routes. The whole process was driven by the public realm from the start."

Just as with Brindleyplace, Argent's plan for Piccadilly Place in Manchester had been about creating a natural route for people to walk through the area. "Cities need navigation," David Partridge says. "You need to lead people by the nose and make it obvious that this is where you go."

Although the site was right opposite Manchester's main railway station, the road network made it a difficult and dangerous journey for pedestrians to get there. "The flow of the city was blocked," Partridge explains. "It is rather like the principle of energy flow that lies behind Chinese medicine and martial arts. You need to identify the urban energy flows – where they are intense and where they eddy away."

The answer was to build a pedestrian bridge from the station, over the main street, through into Piccadilly Place. "It immediately opened up a brand new bit of a city. The impact was phenomenal in the way people moved. We were forming new pedestrian pathways and new pedestrian routes."

Argent became expert in the creation of so-called pedestrian 'desire lines', circuits that guide people from one part of the city to another.

"What we were looking to do in Manchester was connect clusters of activity." Sir Howard Bernstein wanted Argent's help in joining up the distinct commercial and residential districts of the city. "The result was the re-planning of the core and that's been hugely successful because the economic boundaries of the city on the back of that work have been massively expanded, particularly to the north. The momentum of change is continuing."

Argent recognised that the value of its assets in Piccadilly Place and Piccadilly Gardens up the road would increase if people felt comfortable moving between the two. The main route, however, had narrow pavements and numerous bus stops making progress slow and unappealing.

"We persuaded the city not to spend money on a whole series of crossings to the tree-lined central reservation," Partridge recalls. "Instead, we suggested they take the trees out, widen the pavement and replant the trees on the edge of the pavement between the bus stops."

The result was dramatic. Cafés and bars on Piccadilly spilled out onto the wider pavement, setting up tables and chairs for customers to sit out, but leaving ample room for people to stroll along the elegant tree-lined curve of the road.

"Suddenly, we created a more European boulevard," Partridge says. "It is a meeting point of the public and private realms and people love it."

The art of gently manipulating people through a city was vital to the success of Granary Square in London, encouraging the thousands of passengers arriving at King's Cross and St Pancras stations to walk up the hill and discover its delights.

The solution had its origin in one of the lectures in St Andrew's Courthouse. "We had a fascinating lesson in perspectival planning," Robert Evans remembers.

The Ancient Romans believed a city should provide a spectacular setting for the daily life of its citizens - designed in a way that inspires surprise and wonder. The forums in Rome and Pompeii are examples of what became known as scenography or 'view-planning'. "What the Romans were so good at was the unexpected. You go down a narrow alley, through a gap and … wow! We wanted King's Cross to amaze people in the same way."

In designing King's Boulevard, linking the station and the square, Argent needed it to be direct and yet they deliberately gave it a crank at the end.

"The reason it is cranked is to draw you up the hill without immediately revealing your destination," Evans explains. "As you turn at the top, suddenly there is Granary Square in front of you – bang!"

The design of the square itself was the product of all Argent had learned from its work in Birmingham and Manchester. Like Central Square in Brindleyplace and the Piccadilly Place piazza in Manchester, Granary Square includes water features and terraced steps. But this is on a quite different scale. Over a thousand choreographed fountains, each individually lit, have quickly become an attraction by day and night; on a warm afternoon, the wide steps down to the restored canal are almost lost beneath the bodies of contented visitors.

"They have done a blinding job with Granary Square. I think the whole bit by the canal is fascinating," says London Mayor, Boris Johnson. "If only every developer started off with a consideration of the public space."

The idea that a private company should design, build and manage public space is, of course, controversial. There are countless examples of development where streets and squares, nominally part of the open public realm, are actually tightly regulated spaces patrolled by private security guards and protected by barbed wire and anti-climb paint.

Among Argent's ten principles was a commitment to 'promote accessibility'. King's Cross would be 'welcoming and inclusive', helping to make the area 'a real place'.

The London Mayor at the time, Ken Livingstone, had challenged Madelin on what public space meant. "Ken asked me would he be able to demonstrate on Granary Square if he wanted," Madelin recalls. "I said, 'yes', and he said, 'That's all right then'."

The square has already been the location for street protest. "There's a guy who regularly comes up here and goes up on our viewing platform with his loud hailer to criticise the fact that a private company is managing public space," Nick Searl points out. "We don't mind. He rather makes our point for us."

On another occasion, a convoy of naked cyclists made their particular point by wheeling around the area. It raised eyebrows but the security staff did not intervene.

"We have told our security people they are part of the hospitality industry – to think of this as a hotel and the public as our guests," Searl says. Their uniforms are deliberately informal. "Instead of peaked caps or high vis jackets, they wear baseball caps and fleeces."

It is one aspect of a determined effort to encouraging a sense of welcome and belonging. Argent insists that no security barriers should be visible from the street when passers-by look into the office buildings. "If people see barriers everywhere they turn, it makes them feel that a place has nothing to do with them. It appears defensive."

The same principle applies to the boundaries of the project. Far from installing barriers, Argent don't want people even to notice when they cross into the development. "In fifty years, time you shouldn't be able to look at this place and know exactly where the edge was," Robert Evans explains. "It is not about landing a spaceship, it is about being part of something."

Other developers take a different view. Some insist on having their own road signs and paving materials to differentiate their development from the surrounding area. With King's Cross, however, Argent is using Camden Council signage and the Council has the option to adopt the principal streets.

"Camden persuaded us that the civic, municipal interest should permeate the development along trafficked streets," Evans explains. "It's part of being authentic. At the same time, we persuaded them that we are best placed to manage public spaces such as Granary Square and run events within them, with key public rights enshrined in the planning agreement. It works."

Creating successful public space also requires consideration of the private realm within and around it. With the Water's Edge development at Brindleyplace in Birmingham, Argent was keen that the shops, cafés and bars given access to the canal-side development should be local independents – emphasising the contract with the surrounding city rather than giant corporate chains.

"We signed 25 year leases with local firms and we thought it was a good thing, but we were naïve or the world was changing or a bit of both," Roger Madelin suggests. "One bar was offered £1m by a big brewer to assign them the lease and suddenly we had no control at all."

Other independents cashed in and the character of the waterside development changed for a number of years. An area that had been seen as family-friendly became a no-go zone for many on a Friday and Saturday night. "We learned the hard way that if you are in for the long-term, then you have to retain control over the process," Madelin argues.

Nevertheless, Argent's commitment to shaping an area's character by controlling its commercial face is evident elsewhere within the Brindleyplace development. A contemporary art venue, the Ikon Gallery, managed to raise the funds to move into a 19th century former school building on Oozells Square. It was an impressive location on one of the key public spaces, but an American burger giant also wanted the site.

"We were offered a lot of rent by a burger company to turn down the Ikon and build them a restaurant instead," says Madelin. "So the question was would we forego making hundreds of thousands of pounds to get an amazing modern art gallery that was plugged into the city scene? From our point of view, it was a no-brainer."

Argent calculated that, although the gallery would bring in less in rent than the burger joint, it more than made up for it by attracting new types of people to Brindleyplace and in giving the whole area a style and character that increased its overall value. It was also a statement of Argent's commitment to its principles and to the city.

In Manchester, Argent's development of an old car park required a similar calculation – and a bit of creative thinking. The site in the city's trendy Northern Quarter had been identified as a possible home for the Arts Council, and the council regarded them as perfect tenants to enhance the area's Bohemian credentials. The problem for Argent was that the figures didn't quite add up. It was 2008 and the scheme was on the verge of being mothballed.

"I met Sir Howard Bernstein in a restaurant in Cannes at the MIPIM property conference and we did a clever piece of financial engineering," David Partridge explains. "We would sell him the freehold and he would lease it back to us with a 5% gearing." The Argent board went along with the plan and today The Hive is not only the HQ of the Arts Council, but a development with a patina of cool.

"It has been a huge success," Sir Howard calculates. "You have to be commercially intelligent without being commercially mad. It's about utilising parts of your toolkit."

"It feels really quite trendy now," Partridge agrees. "There's a real buzz around The Bakerie Bar which is famous for its artisan breads and wine, there's low-cost office space for creative start-ups and the whole place feels like Shoreditch did when it was reinventing itself."

When it came to Granary Square, Argent exploited all the expertise it had gained in Manchester and Birmingham to turn it into one of London's most vibrant and dynamic spaces. Convincing the Central Saint Martins College of Art and Design to move into Granary Buildings proved to be a master stroke.

"With five-and-a-half thousand of the world's brightest, most visually exciting students on our square, we imported cool," says Roger Madelin. "They don't shuffle along the street in grey suits and brown shoes, they stride and bounce and strut and chat and meander and they do all sorts of things that are unusual for a business environment. It is just brilliant."

Having the rather maverick restaurant Caravan on the square was also seen as important for setting the mood.

"People come to King's Cross for Caravan. It's original, high quality and accessible," Robert Evans believes. "Caravan and its neighbour Grain Store have helped set a certain tone that is very appealing. But those deals are hard work. You're working with passionate entrepreneurs and we have needed to support their investment with innovative deals. We could have done a deal with Costa or Pizza Express or McDonald's much more quickly."

Argent learned a lesson in Brindleyplace and has ensured it retains control of the retail environment. That said, the Birmingham development also taught them the need to leave room for anarchy.

"Looking back now, Brindleyplace is slightly sanitised, it lacks human rough edges," admits David Partridge. "Without a major road going through the development, it ended up being a little over-controlled in the way it is managed."

City developments that are masterplanned within a tight regulatory framework can start to feel artificial. When authenticity is sacrificed in the name of control, that creates places that resemble Disneyland or feel like the constructed reality of the town in the film 'The Truman Show'.

The government had also identified the danger. "Improving our public space is not about creating a sanitised, sterile, shrink-wrapped world," the Deputy Prime Minister, Labour's John Prescott wrote. "It is about creating living, sustainable and inclusive communities – communities where people feel they have a stake in their future."

Argent's answer was to operate to urban design guidelines rather than a rule book. "You want to allow for serendipity, the grit in the oyster," argues Robert Evans. "Developers can be tempted to try to microdesign everything and you can get rather sanitised results. There is something in knowing when to stop."

It is a philosophy one hears again and again from the partners at Argent, "Getting yourself comfortable with chaos is important", as Nick Searl puts it.

"All the ideas of public realm, of moving people, making places to stay, widening pavements, greening with trees, activities on the ground floor, transport there but not dominant - we tried to bring all of the lessons learned and take them to King's Cross," David Partridge explains. "And I think we have made an authentic place."

King's Cross is far from complete, but already people are convinced Argent has achieved the lasting new place they promised. Camden council's former leader Jane Roberts says she was one of the first to sign up to buy a home on the site. "We put a deposit down in 2013 and move in at the end of 2016," she says. "I want to live here because I really like it."

Boris Johnson is also enthusiastic about what is happening in King's Cross. "The whole area is going whoomph! I congratulate Argent on what they have done – I think they had a brilliant vision and they have done it with a meticulous eye for detail," Johnson reckons. "It is going to be a great place to live. If I had a bob or two and I was thinking where I would buy a flat to live in my retirement – King's Cross would be the spot. I think it is going to be 'the place'."

Summer sun, light and shade - Granary Square

CHAPTER 7

MEANING IT

Among the crowds that flock to enjoy the magic of Granary Square are some trying to work out how the trick is done. Just as students and professionals went in their minibuses to Brindleyplace fifteen years ago, their successors stroll up the kinked boulevard from King's Cross and St. Pancras stations to gawp and to wonder.

As they climb the hill, they notice a new entrance to the tube station on the left-hand side. "Quite a cool tunnel," says Robert Evans. With a cool price tag. "Anything we can do psychologically to bring our part of King's Cross closer to the underground symbol, all of us believe that is important."

On the right-hand side, behind boards telling the stories of King's Cross, is where Google will build their UK headquarters. A team from the Internet giant made the same journey up King's Boulevard, ate brunch in Caravan and got blown away by the cool. Indeed, CEO Larry Page has now demanded his architects be more ambitious. London's Mayor is delighted.

"We also want things that are done with a certain amount of confidence and oomph," Boris Johnson says. "If you are going to do a great scheme like King's Cross, there's no point in going in half-measures. You might as well be bold. This is the greatest city on earth going through a fantastic time."

The whole area fizzes with potential. The German Gymnasium, where budding 19th century Olympians once practised Indian club swinging and broadsword fighting, is being redeveloped as a brasserie and bar, wrapped like a birthday present waiting for its big day.

Louis Vuitton fashionistas have moved in to David Chipperfield's elegant boulevard building, with its cast iron columns echoing the gasholders that once dominated the area. Nearby, interactive public art intrigues passengers spilling from trains, as the queue at the meatball van is entertained by a white-faced juggler.

Few consider the complexity of the space they are in: bounded by two huge restored railway terminals, each trying to outshine the other with shops and restaurants and luxury hotels; an underground station straddling six tube lines, vast tunnels beneath their feet extending across the capital and on to the continent; taxis and lorries bringing people and goods in and out; the building sites behind the hoardings – and yet, amid the mayhem, people stop to draw breath here.

"This was the most complicated bit of King's Cross – a huge logistical challenge," Robert Evans says, surveying the scene. "We needed a choreography that was agreed by everyone. I think, in the end, we have got a successful space."

It is Argent's ability to work with partners in a shared ambition to create successful spaces, expertise developed over two decades of major urban regeneration work, which has made the company the most respected name in city development.

It is still busy in Birmingham, working with Hermes and the BT Pension Scheme (its long term backer) and Sir Albert Bore on Paradise Circus, a city centre development of offices, shops, leisure and cultural facilities together with civic amenities, a hotel and new public realm. Expect a water feature, too!

"Argent was brave enough years ago to start acquiring interests in Paradise Circus and, for us, having to negotiate with one developer has its advantages and we've now been able to bring that forward on a joint venture basis," Sir Albert explains.

In Manchester, too, Argent has maintained a strong relationship with Sir Howard Bernstein and is involved in major development work. St. Peter's Square, like Paradise Circus in Birmingham, is an important civic location in the heart of the city, and its refurbishment draws on all of Argent's expertise in creating partnerships to deliver stunning public space.

"It's another example of how Argent initially, and others, came together to create an overarching plan," Sir Howard believes. "They have given business confidence, given investors confidence and the city confidence that over the next few years we'll see a transformed area."

"We are the go-to developer for the public sector because they trust us," David Partridge explains. "They realise we understand the pressures they are under and the aspirations they have. And we have a track record of working with them to achieve those aspirations."

Argent is also involved in Manchester's Airport City project; an £800m property development that Sir Howard hopes will become a globally connected business destination.

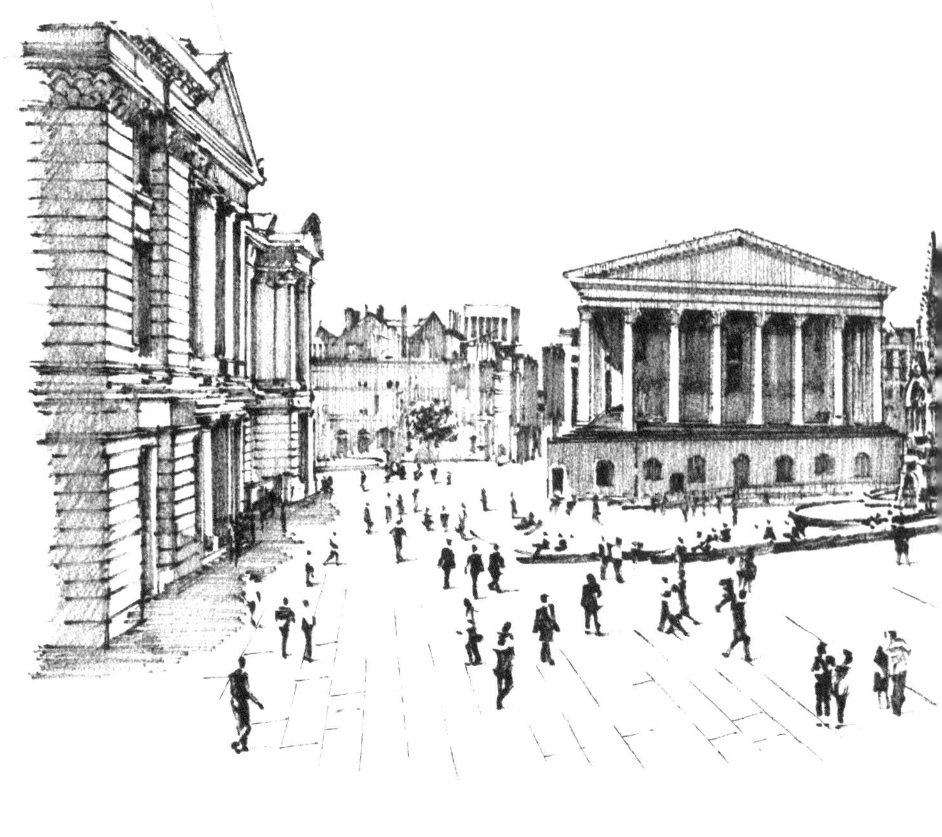

Past, present and future plans - Chamberlain Square, Paradise Circus

"It is a good example of how you must build in resilience," Sir Howard says. "We don't always agree about everything but we sit down and we work it all out. I think Argent's relationship with Manchester and other cities is a testament to how relationships can be made to work for the long term."

It is the commitment to the long term that is the key to understanding Argent's success in Birmingham, Manchester and King's Cross. There have been occasions when the company could have made itself more money by getting out earlier, but Argent is quick to deny there is anything philanthropic behind its motivation. The company sincerely believes that making great lasting places is inherently valuable.

The great renaissance of England's cities, an under-recognised achievement of the last 25 years, has been driven by vision and invention, principle and passion. The heroes of this urban triumph are people who opened their eyes to the challenge and their minds to the possibilities.

The task could not be done alone. Fundamental to success were partnerships, often unfamiliar alliances that could only thrive in an atmosphere of mutual trust.

Many of those who have worked with Argent commend it for its expertise and its integrity; a business that understands the importance of honouring commitments especially during the tough times. That is, perhaps, why it has become the go-to developer in its field. That is why it has become a key player in the urban renaissance. Its philosophy chimes with its ambition.

It recognises that honesty and fidelity are the parents of authenticity.

MEANING IT

ABOUT ARGENT

Argent delivers major commercial, residential, education, cultural and community developments in the UK's largest cities.

City-scale mixed use development is Argent's particular strength. It is involved in the full development process – from identifying and assembling sites, developing designs and obtaining planning permission through to financing, project management of the construction process, letting, asset management and (sometimes) selling. It also manages and maintains buildings and estates.

Argent (Property Development) Services LLP is a limited liability partnership. The partners own the business, which is run by a senior team of ten:

ROBERT EVANS ANDRE GIBBS
TONY GIDDINGS JAMES HEATHER
MIKE LIGHTBOUND ROGER MADELIN
RICHARD MEIER DAVID PARTRIDGE *Managing Partner*
JIM PROWER NICK SEARL

Many of the partners have been working together for more than ten years.

Non-Executive Chairmen:

GEORGE STEER *1988 – 1997*
JOHN SADLER *1997 – 2001*
PETER HAZELL *2001 – 2014*
JONATHAN THOMPSON *from 2014*

Founders (now Non-Executive Directors):

MICHAEL FREEMAN
PETER FREEMAN

HISTORY

1981 Argent is founded by Michael and Peter Freeman.

1994 Argent floats on London Stock Exchange for £150 million.

1997 British Telecom Pension Scheme (BTPS) purchases Argent for £240 million and takes the company private.
Argent's investment portfolio is transferred to BTPS, managed by Hermes. Argent's developments to be carried out in a series of partnerships with Argent's founders and executives.

2012 Argent undergoes internal reorganisation to establish an LLP, to carry on its development and asset management services role.

AWARDS

Since 1994, Argent and its projects have won 87 industry and best practice awards. A selection from the last six years is listed below:

2009 ELISABETH HOUSE, MANCHESTER
Deal of the Year *Awarded by GMPF*

KING'S CROSS, LONDON
National Skills Academy status
Awarded by The National Skills Academy

ARGENT
Property Company of the Year Award - Offices
Awarded by Estates Gazette

ARGENT
Regeneration Award *Awarded by Insider Property Region Awards 2010*

ELEVEN BRINDLEYPLACE, BIRMINGHAM
Best Commercial Workplace *Awarded by BCO Regional Awards*

ARGENT
Developer of the Year *Awarded by Insider Property Region Awards*

2011   KING'S CROSS, LONDON
Regeneration Award *Awarded by Property Week*

THE HIVE, MANCHESTER
Commercial Workplace *Awarded by BCO Regional Awards*

2012   ONE ST. PETER'S SQUARE, MANCHESTER
Commercial Developer of the Year *Awarded by North West Insider Property*

KING'S CROSS, LONDON
RICS Award *Awarded by RICS Awards for London*

KING'S CROSS, LONDON
Best Overall Marketing Campaign (Offices)
Awarded by Property Marketing Awards

ONE ST. PETER'S SQUARE, MANCHESTER
North West Property Deal of the Year
Awarded by North West Inisider Property

KING'S CROSS, LONDON
LABC Award *Awarded by RICS Awards for London*

KING'S CROSS, LONDON
Mayor's Award for Planning Excellence
Awarded by RICS Awards for London

CENTRAL SAINT MARTINS, KING'S CROSS, LONDON
Building of the Year Award *Awarded by AJ100*

2013　　ARGENT
　　　　Developer of the Year *Awarded by Property Awards 2013*

　　　　KING'S CROSS, LONDON
　　　　Deal of the Year - Industry Impact *Awarded by Estates Gazette*

　　　　KING'S CROSS, LONDON
　　　　Regeneration Award *Awarded by Property Awards 2013*

　　　　ARGENT
　　　　Property Firm of the Year *Awarded by City AM*

　　　　ARGENT
　　　　Client of the Year *Awarded by AJ100*

2014 ARGENT OFFICE, 4 STABLE STREET, LONDON
Projects up to 2,000 sq m *Awarded by BCO National Awards*

KINGS CROSS AND ST. PANCRAS BUSINESS
PARTNERSHIP, LONDON
Improvement to Londoners' Quality of Life *Awarded by London First*

KING'S CROSS MASTERPLAN, LONDON
Best of the Best *Awarded by NLA Awards*

ROGER MADELIN & DAVID PARTRIDGE
Property Personality of the Year *Awarded by Property Awards*

ONE PANCRAS SQUARE, KING'S CROSS, LONDON
Commercial category *Awarded by RIBA*

AIRPORT CITY, MANCHESTER
Property Deal of the Year *Awarded by Insider Property Awards*

KING'S CROSS, LONDON
Masterplan *Awarded by NLA Awards*

ROGER MADELIN
New Londoner Award *Awarded by NLA Awards*

KING'S CROSS, LONDON
Deal of the Year *Awarded by Office Agents Society*

CONTACT

Argent (Property Development) Services LLP

4 Stable Street	Eleven Brindleyplace	One Piccadilly Gardens
King's Cross	Brindleyplace	Piccadilly
London	Birmingham	Manchester
N1C 4AB	B1 2LP	M1 1RG
T: +44 20 3664 0200	T: +44 121 643 7799	T: +44 161 236 1878

www.argentllp.co.uk

follow us: @argentllp

"We are proud that every one of our offices is in a development which Argent has created"
David Partridge Managing Partner